Table of Contents

I0016572

iLife

iPhoto

iPhoto is a great way to organize your photos (and videos). You can edit photos, create personal cards, calendars or share one or all of them on the web. As with the other applications, I am going to go over all of the icons that appear on the window and all of the iPhoto menus. A sample of an iPhoto window – showing an event is shown below.

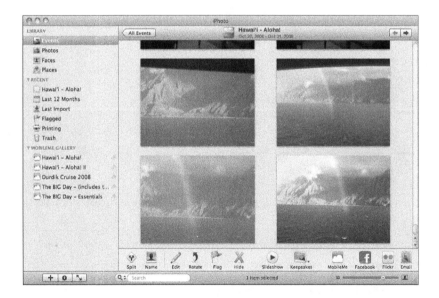

Note: I shrunk the screen so Keepsakes expanded is actually...

If you are launching iPhoto for the first time, there are a few screens you need to go through
to get to the main program. The first
dialog box asks if you want to play a
welcome video, view video tutorials or
how to get hands-on training. This
window is shown to the right. If you do
not need any of these items at this
point, you can just click on the close
button to start having photo fun in iPhoto.

The next is setting up locations in iPhoto. This dialog box is shown below.

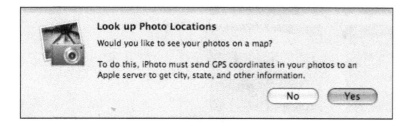

The next item is very important. You are asked if you want iPhoto to run automatically
when you attach a
camera. If you plan to
use iPhoto for your
entire photo needs –
then say Yes and have it

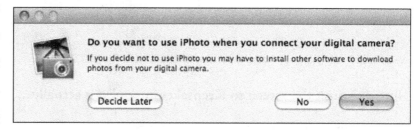

automatically run. The one downside is that it takes time to download the items into the
program if you have a lot of items. If you select No, you can use a card reader and sort out
the photos first before importing them into iPhoto. This window is shown above.

Breakdown of iPhoto Main Window

Library - Events

You can sort your photos into events. This makes it easier to create special personal projects or share them later. In the example above – I have two events – Hawai'i – Aloha! and Hawai'i Aloha II.

Library – Photos

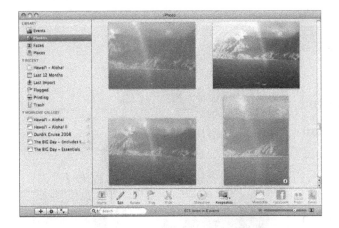

This just views all your photos in one big group. It is recommended to sort them out and create an event with the new photos you added.

Library – Faces

This is a way cool tool introduced in the latest version of iPhoto. The application is trained to pick out faces and have the ability to find them elsewhere in your Library. The first step is for iPhoto to run short setup routine. This is shown to right.

a

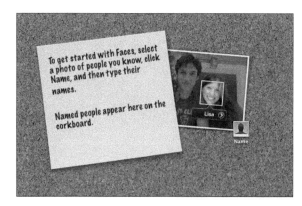

The next screen that is shown is displayed to the left. The note in the middle describes how to activate this feature. An example is shown on the next page.

Next, highlight the photo with the face you want to use and click on the **Name button**

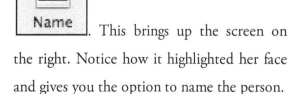

. This brings up the screen on the right. Notice how it highlighted her face and gives you the option to name the person.

After this is done and go to Faces – you will see a picture of the face you named on a corkboard. If you select that person – all (hopefully) of the pictures with that name and face will show up. This is shown above.

Library – Places

Places allows you to give your photo geographic info. You can then view the area as "terrain" or a satellite view. Interesting – No? Here is an example…

1. Chose a picture from you album.
2. Click on the "I" button on the bottom right of the photo.
3. This brings up the following screen…

Click on photo place and highlight – Find on map…

This brings up the screen below. Type in the location (Island, State in this example)

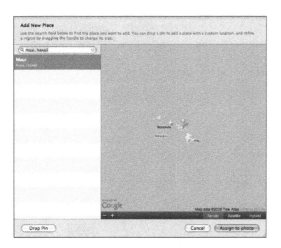

Click on **Assign to photo**. Finished. So – why is this useful? If you have zillions of pictures from family vacations – you can now see on a world map where you been. And once you pick a place on the map – you see all the photos from the location. Example on next page.

Notice that it is now on Satellite mode and I have been to Hawaii and New York. If I click and hold down the mouse on the pin in New York, it will show all the photos from New York (that I tagged as NY of course).

Recent

Simply, this brings up where you have been last, printed last or what is in the trash.

MobileMe

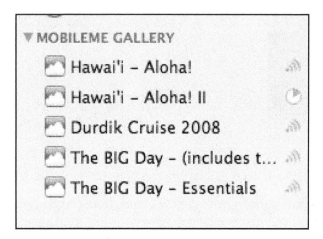

MobileMe allows you to quickly and easily share photos and videos on the web. In the example above, there are five events that I am sharing on web at the moment.

On the bottom right hand corner are two buttons that relate to MobileMe. It looks like this

. **Tell a Friend** just allows you to announce that a new gallery is being shared and gives the link to the new gallery in the email it generates.

Settings – Allows you to change how the gallery interacts with the viewers. This screen is shown below.

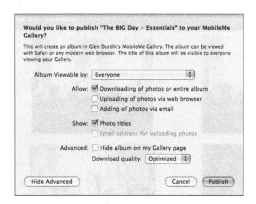

 This button allows you to create various new items in iPhoto. If you click this button – the screen below is brought up.

Note: See where it states Use selected items in new album. Use the select all command to grab all the photos in window. Hold down the $\boxed{\textbf{COMMAND}}$ key while clicking on individual photos to take just the ones you want in the new album (book, card, calendar, slideshow).

 This button brings up basic info on a photo. A sample is shown on the next page.

 This is the **Full Screen button**. Click on it and the photo takes up the whole screen. To get out of it – press the $\boxed{\text{esc}}$ key.

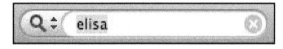 This is the **Search** tool. If the photos are named, you can search for items this way.

Name: Sets a name of a face in the photo

Notice that it thinks it is Elisa based on steps taken earlier. Click on the check mark to confirm.

Edit: Allows you to manipulate your photo in a variety of ways. These items are shown below. **Rotate** – rotates image 90 degrees every click. **Crop** – Highlight an area you want to keep and it removes the rest. **Straighten** – Free rotate the photo to make objects appear "more straight." **Enhance** – iPhoto evaluates your photo and tries to make it look the best it can be. Sometimes great. Sometimes not. **Red-Eye** – removes the red dots in the eyes of people in a photo due to a flash. **Retouch** – tried to remove blemishes from your photo.

Effects – See sample below

Adjust: For the more advanced user – which you should be in no time!

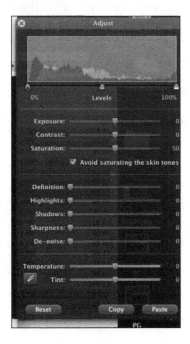

Slideshow: Allows you play a slideshow (automatically displays all selected photos at specific intervals.) If you move your mouse around the bottom middle of the screen, you are given the opportunity to modify the slideshow settings. A black and white toolbar will appear. On the left, you can click the left arrow to go back or the right arrow to move forward. If you click on one of the three icons next to the arrows, you change the theme, music and other settings. This is shown on the previous page.

Book: Want to create the ultimate coffee table book featuring your family? The Book feature allows you to create a professional quality book from the photos you chose. Notice

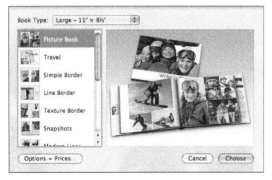

the **Options and Prices button**. This book is created by Apple and this link explains all the details by going to an Apple website.

Here is a sample window of what steps are involved in creating book. This is a picture of the cover. You can choose themes, backgrounds, different layouts, etc. When you are done – click on **Buy Book.**

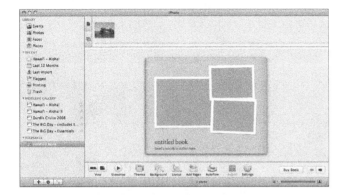

Calendar: Create custom calendars in no time. So now there is no time like the present and make a calendar that has some meaning to you and your family.

Here are some cool notes....

As you see in the example below – you can import iCal calendar events and birthdays (if present) from the Address book.

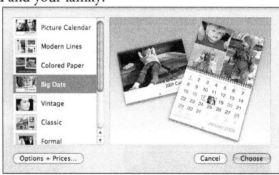

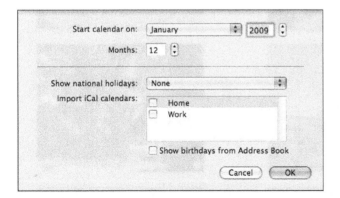

Card: Create your own special sentimental card with your photos here. I have selected Holiday/Events in the example to the right.

 Want the world to see your creative side? This buttons allow you to share your photos four different ways.

MobileMe: Below are all the options available to you when you publish your photos via MobileMe.

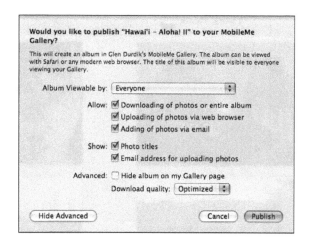

Facebook and **Flickr** are services that allow people to view your personally created websites describing yourself.

Mail: Allows you to send photos via email. Notice in the middle of sample below that you can specify the size of the photo (shrink it down to make it send/retrieved faster.

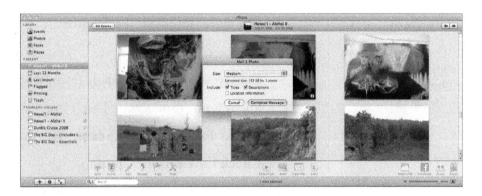

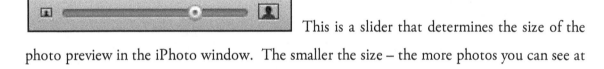 This is a slider that determines the size of the photo preview in the iPhoto window. The smaller the size – the more photos you can see at once. The larger the size – the more detail you can see.

iPhoto Menus

iPhoto – iPhoto Menu

This menu has a few important items. **About iPhoto** tells you what version you have installed. **Preferences...** are discussed in detail next. You can **Empty the iPhoto trash** here or shop for iPhoto products. Last, you can **check for software updates via the Check for Updates... option**.

iPhoto – iPhoto Menu – Preferences – General

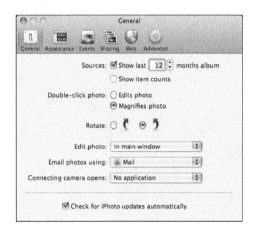

Sources – decide how many months you want to show and decide if you want to show item counts.

Decide whether or not a double-click on a photo edits or magnifies the photo. Decide what direction you want the default rotate to be. You can decide where to edit the photo – Main Window, Full Screen or a separate application all together. You decide how you want to email photos. Last, decide if you want iPhoto, Image Capture or no application to be launched when a camera is connected. Oh, you can have iPhoto automatically check for updates as well.

iPhoto – iPhoto Menu – Preferences – Appearance

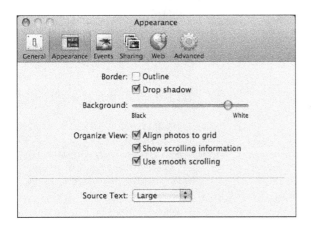

Border - decides whether you want a drop shadow or outline around your photos. **Background** – a slider that sets the color behind you pictures – it goes from all black to all white.

Organize View – the default is to have all three options checked. They are – Align photos to grid, show scrolling info and use smooth scrolling. The last option is to set source text as small or large.

iPhoto – iPhoto Menu – Preferences – Events

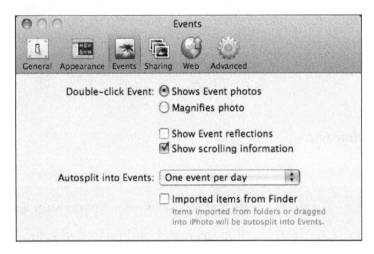

Double-click Event – can be set to either show event photos or magnify photos. **Show event reflections** – adds a reflection of the first event photo on your screen. You can also have iPhoto show scrolling information. **Autosplit into Events** – it can be one event per day, one event per week, two hour gap or an eight hour gap. Last, you check off the box to have items imported from the Finder autosplit.

iPhoto – iPhoto Menu – Preferences – Sharing

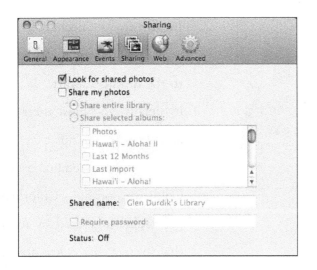

If you are on a local network, you can have iPhoto search for shared photos. This also applies to you – do you want to share your photos (all or part)? If you share your photos – you can give them a name so that other people will recognize them on the network. You can also give it a password as well.

iPhoto – iPhoto Menu – Preferences – Web

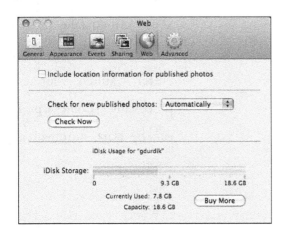

If you added location data to your photos – you can add this to your shared photos. You can check if there are any new published photos. Last, the window shows your iDisk usage and how much space you used and have left. Notice that you have the option to buy more space here as well.

iPhoto – iPhoto Menu – Preferences – Advanced

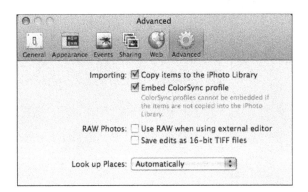

Importing – decide if you want new photos to be added to the iPhoto Library. It is on by default and most users will leave it on. You have the option to embed the ColorSync profile. ColorSync is a technology used by Apple that insures that colors are the same across Macs. There are other standards as well. **RAW Photos** – high-end cameras allow you to take these kinds of photos. These photos are better suited for image processing. **Look up Places** can be done automatically or never.

iPhoto – File Menu

New Album...	⌘N
New Album From Selection...	⇧⌘N
New Smart Album...	⌥⌘N
New Folder	⌥⇧⌘N
Get Info	⌘I
Import to Library...	⇧⌘I
Export...	⇧⌘E
Close Window	⌘W
Edit Smart Album	
Subscribe to Photo Feed...	⌘U
Order Prints...	
Print...	⌘P
Browse Backups...	

New Album – creates a new Album for you. **New Album from Selection** – if you want to create an album from a selected few photos – chose this option. **New Smart Album** – This will create an album based on criteria you set. It could be date, filename, face, place, etc. **New Folder** – creates an empty album. **Get Info** – gives you details on various characteristics of your photo. **Import to Library...** You can use this to take files not already in iPhoto and add them. (You can drag it in as well) **Export** – You can export your photo to a number of formats. These include – JPEG, TIFF, PNG, a web page, QuickTime Movie or slideshow. A slideshow, by default is sent to iTunes. You can subscribe to a photo feed. This is one place to go to if you want to order prints of your photos. **Browse**

Backups... brings up Time Machine. If you accidentally or you child accidentally deleted a great photo – go here to get it back.

iPhoto – Edit Menu

Undo Rotate Photo	⌘Z
Redo	⇧⌘Z
Cut	⌘X
Copy	⌘C
Paste	⌘V
Select All	⌘A
Select None	⇧⌘A
Find	⌘F
Font	▶
Spelling	▶
Special Characters...	

Here you can "**undo**" an action or redo it if you decide to keep the change you made. **Cut** – Deletes what is highlighted. **Copy** – Puts what is highlighted into the Mac's clipboard. **Paste** – Takes what is in the clipboard and puts it into the area you are working on. **Select All** – Highlights all items at once. **Find** – Search iPhoto for a specific item. **Font** – Changes the font you are using. **Spelling** – checks the spelling of the text you have typed. **Special Characters** – gives you access to a window that shows all of the special characters found in each font.

iPhoto – Photo Menu

Show Extended Photo Info	⌥⌘I
Adjust Date and Time...	
Batch Change...	⇧⌘B
Rotate Clockwise	⌥⌘R
Rotate Counter Clockwise	⌘R
My Rating	▶
Flag Photo	⌘.
Hide Photo	⌘L
Duplicate	⌘D
Delete From Album	⌘⌫
Revert to Original	

Show Extended Photo Info – If you are a professional photographer – this item can be very useful as it gives a ton of info on the selected photo. **Adjust Date and Time...** - changes the date and time of the selected photo. **Rotate Clockwise or Counter Clockwise** – does what it says. **My rating** – you can assign ratings for each photo if you wish. **Flag Photo** – tags the photo with a flag and places it in the Flagged photo library as well. **Hide Photo** – Hides the photo from the window. You can go to the View Menu and select Hidden Photos to see them again. **Duplicate** – copies the entire photo and adds the copy to the album. **Delete from album** – deletes the photo from an album. **Revert to original** – Removes all changes done to photo.

iPhoto – Event Menu

Create Event
Create Event From Flagged Photos
Split Event
Make Key Photo
Add Flagged Photos To Selected Event
Open in Separate Window

Autosplit Selected Events

This menu creates events – empty or from flagged photos. **Split Event** – can split an event into smaller sections. **Make Key Photo** – every event has a photo that shows up as the primary photo for the event – the photo you see in the Events Library. **Add Flagged Photos to Selected Event** – moves photos you flagged into an event of your choice.

Open in Separate Window – takes the event and put the photos in a new window – photos cannot be modified. **Autosplit Selected Events** – you can specify what day or time folder you want your imported photos to go into.

iPhoto - Share Menu

```
┌─────────────────────────────────┐
│  Email                          │
│  Set Desktop                    │
│                                 │
│  MobileMe Gallery               │
│  Facebook                       │
│  Flickr                         │
│                                 │
│  Send to iWeb           ▶       │
│  Send to iDVD                   │
│  Burn                           │
└─────────────────────────────────┘
```

This menu allows you to share you photos to the outside world through email, **Facebook**, **Flickr** or via a **MobileMe** gallery. You can set you desktop to be the picture of you choice here as well. You can send it iWeb or iDVD. Last, you can burn the images onto a CD-R.

iPhoto – View Menu

```
┌─────────────────────────────────┐
│  Titles               ⇧⌘T       │
│  Rating               ⇧⌘R       │
│  Keywords             ⇧⌘K       │
│                                 │
│  Event Titles         ⇧⌘F       │
│  Hidden Photos        ⇧⌘H       │
│                                 │
│  Sort Photos            ▶       │
│                                 │
│  Show in Toolbar        ▶       │
│                                 │
│  Full Screen          ⌥⌘F       │
│  Always Show Toolbar            │
│  Thumbnails             ▶       │
└─────────────────────────────────┘
```

This menu allows you to decide what info is displayed with your photo. It allows you to see hidden photos. **Show in Toolbar** – gives you the choice to add other items besides the default ones. Set desktop and printing are two choices.

iPhoto – Window Menu

Minimize	⌘M
Zoom	
Show Keywords	⌘K
Manage My Places	
Bring All to Front	
✓ iPhoto	

Minimize – shrinks the iPhoto window and places it in the dock. To get it back – click on the icon in the dock. **Zoom** – makes the window the largest it can be. **Manage My Places** – If you place location data into the info section of a photo – you can modify the locations here. **Bring All to Front** – If you have many applications open – you can bring all iPhoto windows to the top of the stack of open windows.

iPhoto – Help Menu

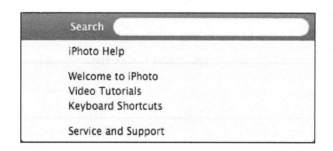

This is the place to go to when you ask, "How do I do that??" My manual is a good primer for users – but this menu covers a lot of items in more detail.

On the count of three…say Cheese!! Now you have a good background on how iPhoto works and all of the great things you can do with it.

iLife

iDVD

iDVD

iDVD makes it very easy to create professional looking DVDs in a flash. If you have time to

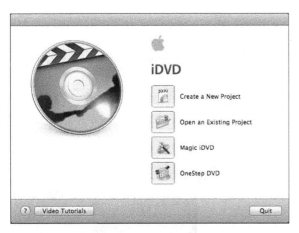

experiment – you can create amazing DVDs – have fun and experiment. iDVD also includes options to create DVDs with just a click of the mouse. To the left is the first screen you see when you launch iDVD. I will cover all the options here as well the toolbars and menus in the coming pages.

If you click on **Create a New Project** – the first options to come up are to name the project

and decide if you want it to be widescreen (large rectangle as opposed to standard which is more square) or not. This is shown to the right.

The next screen is the main workspace for iDVD. This is shown on the next page.

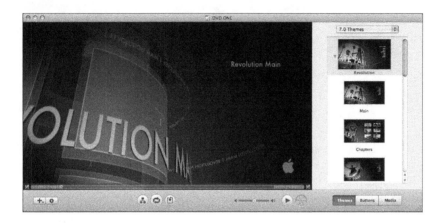

 This button adds a new Submenu, Movie or Slideshow to your project.

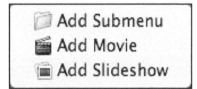

 This button gives you access to info on all aspects of your project. This includes Background, Audio, Buttons and Drop Zones.

This is called the DVD Map. It is a nice way to visualize your project. The main work area is the area to the left where there is a grey box and a blue box. You can add elements here – a most intuitive way to add items.

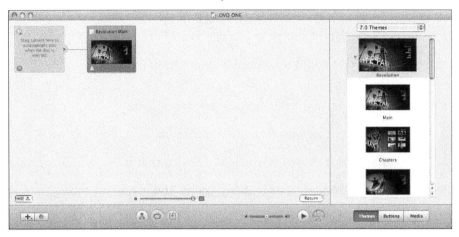

 This button starts or stops motion.

 This button allows you to edit drop zones. An example is shown to the right.

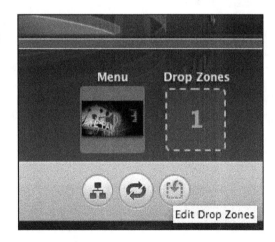

 This slider just controls the volume of playback.

 This button simulates a PLAY of your project.

This button activates the BURN of your project to a DVD. Depending on the amount of media in your project – this could take quite sometime to complete.

On the far right of the screen – you will see three buttons. They are Themes, Buttons and Media. The first button – **Themes** is shown to the left. Notice that it states 7.0 themes. This is actually a drop down menu and gives you access to earlier themes as well.

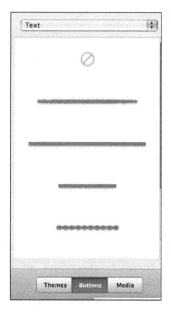

The next is **Buttons**. This allows you to add one of the available icons to an added submenu for example.

The last button is **Media.** This gives you access to all of your media files found in **iPhoto**, **iTunes** or an **iMovie** movie file.

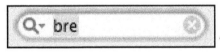 This item found in the media window allows you to search files that meet your criteria.

iDVD – Menus

iDVD - iDVD Menu

This contains a few important items. **About iDVD** – tells you what version you are running. **Check for Updates...** goes online to check to see if there are updates. **Preferences...** are discussed in detail below.

iDVD – iDVD Menu – Preferences – General

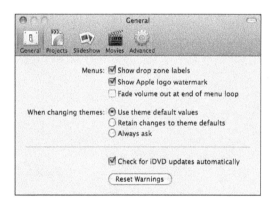

This menu window allows you to specify if menus show drop zone labels, decide if you want to show the Apple logo watermark or fade volume out at the end of a menu loop. If you change themes – you can specify it to use theme default values, retain changes to theme defaults or always ask. Here you can have iDVD always check for updates.

iDVD – iDVD Menu – Preferences – Projects

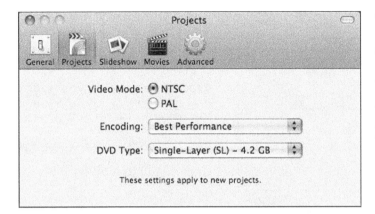

Video Mode: North America and Europe have different standards. NTSC is the default – which is North America. **Encoding** - you can chose between Best Performance, High Quality or Professional Quality. **DVD Type** – specifies what type of DVD you use – Single Layer (most common) or Double Layer

iDVD – iDVD Menu – Preferences – Slideshow

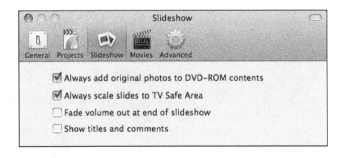

Here you have four options when creating slides. They are: decide if you always wan to add original photos to DVD-ROM contents (should leave on), always scale slides to TV Safe Area, fade volume put at the end of a slideshow and if you want to show titles and comments.

iDVD – iDVD Menu – Preferences – Movies

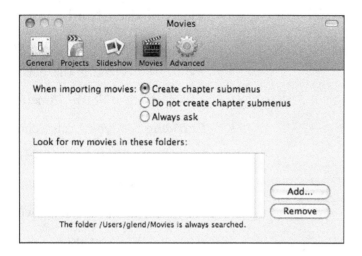

There are two basic questions asked here. One – when you import a movie – do you want it to create a chapter submenu or not. Second – where do you want iDVD to look for movies.

iDVD – iDVD Menu – Preferences – Advanced

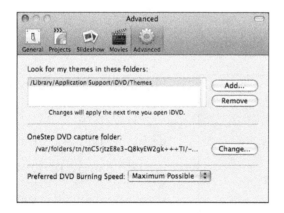

The first option is to set where your themes are located. The one in the window to the left is the default one. You can add others if you like. **OneStep** is discussed later. The **Preferred DVD Burning Speed** is set to Maximum possible by default. You can it to a slower speed if you prefer.

iDVD – File Menu

New...	⌘N
Open...	⌘O
Open Recent	▶
Magic iDVD...	
OneStep DVD	
OneStep DVD from Movie...	
Close Window	⌘W
Save	⌘S
Save As...	⇧⌘S
Archive Project...	
Save Theme as Favorite...	
Import	▶
Burn DVD...	⌘R
Save as Disc Image...	⇧⌘R
Save as VIDEO_TS folder...	

Here you can create a new project, open a save project or open a recently opened project. You can also **Save** or perform a **Save As...** here as well. You can **Burn a DVD** here, **Save it as a Disc Image** or **VIDEO_TS folder**.

iDVD – File Menu - Magic iDVD...

Magic iDVD takes out a lot of the planning out of making a new DVD. You enter a title, choose a theme, drag in movies and photos and instant DVD project file is created.

iDVD – File Menu – OneStep DVD

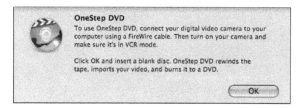

This option is very simple. Connect your video camera via Firewire. Turn it on and set it to VCR mode. Insert a blank DVD. Click on OK. Videotape to DVD in no time flat. No bells and whistles, but fast.

iDVD – Edit Menu

Undo Add Movie	⌘Z
Redo	⇧⌘Z
Cut	⌘X
Copy	⌘C
Paste	⌘V
Paste and Match Style	⌥⇧⌘V
Delete	
Duplicate	⌘D
Copy Style	⌥⌘C
Paste Style	⌥⌘V
Select All Buttons	⌘A
Select None	⇧⌘A
Special Characters...	

Here you can **undo** or **redo** a recent change. You can **Cut** items out, **Copy** them or after copied, **Paste** them into your project somewhere else. You can **Delete** or **Duplicate** elements of you project. You can **Select All Buttons** if you wish. You also have access to **Special Characters...** as well. These are unique symbols or graphics not normally seen when you access a font.

iDVD - Project Menu

Project Info...	⇧⌘I
Switch to Standard (4:3)	⌥⌘A
Edit Drop Zones	
Autofill Drop Zones...	⇧⌘F
Add Submenu	⇧⌘N
Add Movie	⇧⌘O
Add Slideshow	⌘L
Add Text	⌘K
Add Title Menu Button	
New Menu from Selection	
Go Back	⌘B

Project Info... Shown on Next Page. You can switch your DVD back or forth form Standard to Widescreen. You can **Edit Drop zones** here. You can add a **Submenu**, **Movie**, **Slideshow**, **Text** or **Title Menu Button**.

iDVD - Project Menu – Project Info...

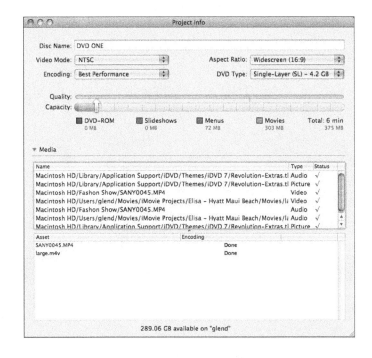

This gives you all the important data in regards to your project.

iDVD – View Menu

Motion	⌘J
Show Map	⇧⌘M
Show Inspector	⌘I
Hide Motion Playhead	
Show TV Safe Area	⌘T
Show Standard Crop Area	⌥⌘T

In this menu – you can determine what tools are to been seen on your screen.

iDVD – Advanced Menu

```
Apply Theme to Project
Apply Theme to Submenus

Reset Object to Theme Settings

✓ Loop movie
Create Chapter Markers for Movie

✓ Encode in Background
Delete Encoded Assets

Edit DVD-ROM Contents...
```

In this menu – you decide if you want to apply a theme to a Project or to Submenus. You can have it set to encode items in the background. You can also delete already encoded assets. Last, you can edit DVD-ROM Contents.

iDVD – Window Menu

```
Minimize          ⌘M
Zoom

Actual Size       ⌘1
Fit to Screen

Bring All to Front
```

Here you can **Minimize** a window to the dock or **Zoom** the screen to its largest size. You can also set it the screen to its **Actual size** or **Fit to screen**. If you have a lot of programs open, you can bring all windows related to iDVD to the top by selecting – **Bring All to Front.**

iDVD – Help Menu

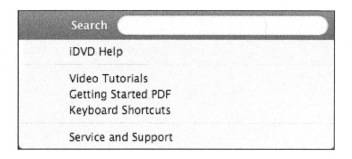

This menu allows you to search for help on items, access Video Tutorials, or the Getting Started PDF. You also have access to a list of keyboard shortcuts.

That's iDVD. Ready to become the next Hollywood Mogul? Have fun trying out new things and share you wonderful events with everyone.

iLife

iMovie

iMovie is a great program. It can be used with just a learning a few basic steps or it can involve a lot of complicated additions to help make a good movie a great movie. As with the other guides – I just want to go over the very basics of the program. Learn where everything is located via this manual. Sit down and explore for a few minutes or hours and learn to become a great video editor. That being said, let's begin… The first screen you encounter is the Welcome screen. As with the other applications – you have access to online tutorials or welcome video to help get you started. Click on the close button to begin creating the next blockbuster.

On the next page is the Main Screen of iMovie. It consists of three parts. They are the **Preview Window, Project Window and Event Window.** I used iMovie a few months ago to edit them and post them via **MobileMe** on the Internet.

Project

Window

Preview

Window

Event

Window

Notice in the example above, there is no project in the **Project Window**. If I drag an event from the **Event window** – I am asked to create a new Project. This is shown to the right. Here you must give it a name, decide if it is

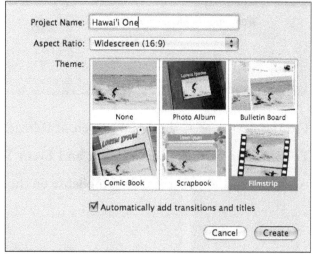

Widescreen or Standard and choose a Theme. You can have it also automatically add transitions and titles if you prefer.

Project Window Buttons

The button on the far left plays the video at full screen. The button next to it plays the video from the beginning.

This tells you the time of the video in the Project window. (I imported a short video after taking the screenshot of the main window above.)

iMovie shows a "picture" of moments in your video to show a preview of the entire video. In the example here – this picture occurs every 5 seconds until the end of the clip.

Below Project Window

Camera Import Button. If you have an iSight camera – this will pop up when you click on it. If you attach a video camera this will show up as well. The sample window is shown to the left. Click on **Capture...** to begin recording. Click on **Done** to return to iMovie.

 Swap Project Window with

Event Window. In my example – Project is on top and Event is on the bottom. You can reverse the two if you prefer.

This slider determines the size of the snapshot pictures of your clip(s) or complete movie.

If you want to add a short highlighted clip to your project – highlight the frames and click on this button. This adds the selection to you project.

The first star marks the highlighted clip as a Favorite. The second – hollow star "unmarks" the selection. The X button rejects the clip and deletes it from the complete clip.

This button allows you to add a Voiceover to your clip(s).

If you just want a certain area of your clip to be on the screen – use this tool called Crop. You could just have a video cropped to show one face in a large crowd for example.

This is the **Inspector button**. It gives you a nice summary of the clip. This is shown to the right.

 This feature shows you the left and right volume of the sound in your clip(s).

 This button allows you to show the music and sound effects window. This is shown to the right. Note that is has access to your **iTunes Library, iLife Sound Effects and iMovie Sound Effects.**

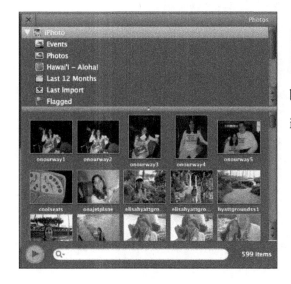 This button brings up the **Photo browser**. This is shown to the left. Notice that it brings up iPhoto items.

This button brings up the **Title browser**. This is shown to the right.

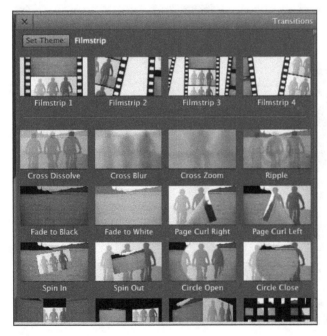

This button brings up the **Transitions browser**. The options available are shown to the left.

This button brings up the **Map and Background** browser. The options available are shown to the right.

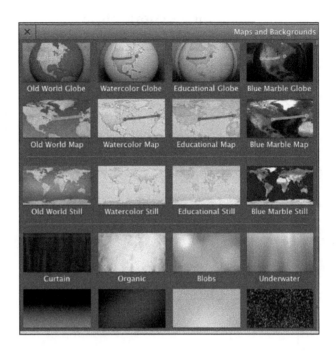

 This button deals with Events. In the example of the main window I used at the beginning of this guide - there is a list of events on the left and to the right of that – the actual clips with the snapshot pictures. If you click this button – the text part of the Event window will disappear and leave just the clips showing.

This also deals with Events. You have the choice of Favorites and Unmarked, Favorites only, All clips or Rejected ones.

iMovie Menus

iMovie – iMovie Menu

About iMovie
Preferences...   ⌘,
Shop for iMovie Products
Provide iMovie Feedback
Register iMovie
Check for Updates...
Hide iMovie   ⌘H
Hide Others   ⌥⌘H
Show All
Quit iMovie   ⌘Q

This menu contains a few important items. **About iMovie** - tells you what version you are running. You can further down – check for updates manually. **Preferences...** are discussed below.

iMovie – iMovie Menu – Preferences - General

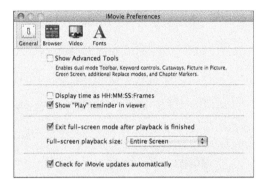

The first option asks if you want to show **Advanced Tools**. These include Cutaways, Picture in Picture, Green Screen and a few others. Not for the more casual user. You can display time as HH:MM:SS:Frames. You can have the "Play" reminder in viewer, set if you want to exit full-screen mode after playback is finished. You can set Full-screen to entire screen, double, actual or half. Last, you can set iMovie to check for updates automatically.

iMovie – iMovie Menu – Preferences - Browser

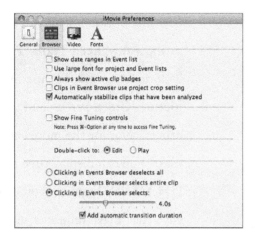

This menu is broken down into four sections. The first section on top allows you to show date ranges in the Event list, Use large font for project and Event lists, decide if you want to always show active clip badges, decide if you want clips in the Event browser to use project crop settings and last – automatically stabilize clips that have been analyzed. The second section asks if you want to show Fine Tuning controls. The third section asks what to do with a double-click – Edit or Play. The last section deals with mouse clicking on various items in iMovie.

iMovie – iMovie Menu – Preferences - Video

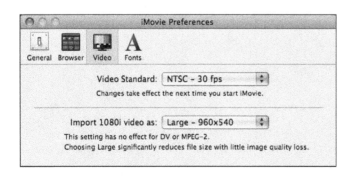

Video Standard – Can be NTSC or PAL. Every region has different standard. The U.S. uses NTSC. You can also set what happens when you import HD video – large or Full.

iMovie – iMovie Menu – Preferences - Fonts

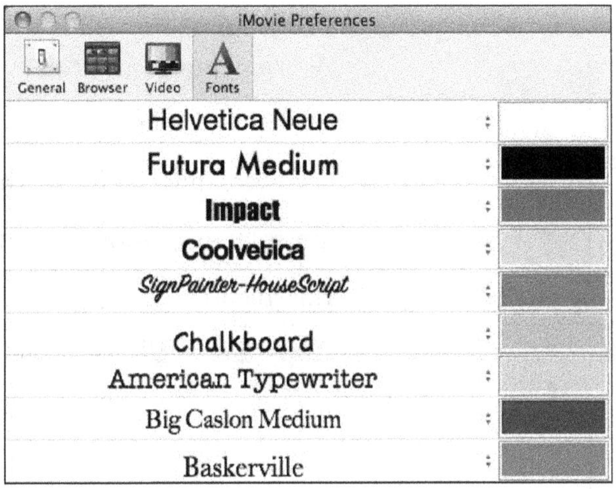

This menu sets the color and Font combinations. You are not limited to the fonts shown to the left. Click on the two small arrows to change the font.

iMovie – File Menu

Here you can create a **New Project or Event**. Check out Project Properties. **Space Saver** moves rejected clips to the Trash. You can also print an event if you wish.

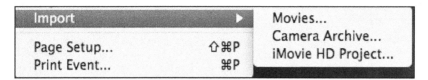

Import options found in the File Menu.

iMovie – Edit Menu

Undo Change Title	⌘Z
Redo	⇧⌘Z
Cut	⌘X
Copy	⌘C
Paste	⌘V
Paste Adjustments	▶
Reject Selection	⌫
Reject Entire Clip	⌥⌫
Select Entire Clip	⌘A
Select	▶
Trim to Selection	⌘B
Trim Clip End	▶
Split Clip	⇧⌘S
Join Clip	
Detach Audio	
Mute Clip	⇧⌘M
Reveal in Event Browser	
Arrange Music Tracks...	
Unpin Music Track	
Add Beat Marker	M
Spelling	▶
Special Characters...	⌥⌘T

As this program deals with adding or deleting items to achieve a final movie – there are a lot of options found in this menu. **Trim** and **Trim Clip End** allows you to remove unwanted footage in your movie. You can **Split** clips as well as **Join** Clips in this menu. There is section dealing with audio at the bottom of this menu. You can **Arrange Music Tracks**, "**Unpin a Music Track**" (which allows you to remove it and rearrange the tracks again) and **Add a Beat Marker.**

iMovie - View Menu

Favorites Only	
✓ Favorites and Unmarked	⌘L
All Clips	
Rejected Only	
Group Events By Disk	
Group Events By Month	
✓ Most Recent Events at Top	
Show Separate Days in Events	
Play	space
Play Selection	/
Play from Beginning	\
Play Around Current Frame	▶
Play full-screen	⌘G
✓ Snap to Ends	
✓ Snap to Beats	⌘U
✓ Audio Skimming	⌘K
Playhead Info	⌘Y

This menu allows you great control over how items are viewed. There are five options for Play for example.

iMovie – Text Menu

Show Fonts	⌘T
Bold	⇧⌘B
Italic	⇧⌘I
Underline	⇧⌘U
Outline	⇧⌘O
Bigger	⌘+
Smaller	⌘−
Align	▶
Kern	▶
Ligature	▶
Baseline	▶
Copy Style	⌥⌘C
Paste Style	⌥⌘V

This menu deals exclusively with fonts. It gives you control over changing various characteristics.

iMovie - Share Menu

```
iTunes...
iDVD
Media Browser...
YouTube...
MobileMe Gallery...

Export Movie...                    ⌘E
Export using QuickTime...
Export Final Cut XML...

Remove from iTunes
Remove from Media Browser...
Remove from MobileMe Gallery...
Remove from YouTube...
```

Show your work to the world! Here you can **send it to iTunes or iDVD**. Share it on the Internet via **YouTube** or **MobileMe**. **Final Cut** is a truly professional application far more advanced then iMovie.

iMovie – Window Menu

```
Minimize                           ⌘M
Minimize All
Zoom

Precision Editor                   ⌘/
Clip Trimmer                       ⌘R

Clip Adjustments                   I
Video Adjustments                  V
Audio Adjustments                  A
Cropping, Ken Burns & Rotation     C

Show Projects full-screen          ⌘6
Show Events full-screen            ⌘7

Show Project Library
Hide Event Library
Viewer                             ▶
Swap Events and Projects

Music and Sound Effects            ⌘1
Photos                             ⌘2
Titles                             ⌘3
Transitions                        ⌘4
Maps and Backgrounds               ⌘5
```

This menu gives you a ton of options as to what you want to see when editing a movie clip. Clip, Video, Audio adjustments or the Music and Sound effect browser, photo browser, etc.

iMovie – Help Menu

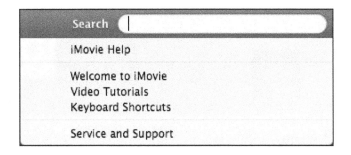

There is A LOT to learn to effectively use this program. Use this guide to get started. Access the features of this menu for further advice and guidance.

Remember me when you win you first Academy award!! I hope I helped explain this complex program in these few pages. Now you know where everything is located – start shooting video and make the next Blockbuster!

iLife

iWeb

iWeb is a great way to start learning how to create awesome websites. With its ease of use and powerful tools – you can create a spectacular website in no time. As with the other "i"

applications – iWeb starts out with a Welcome screen that allows you to access a getting started video or video tutorials. Use my guide to get your feet wet and Explore! Explore! Explore!

If you click on close on the Welcome screen – iWeb will bring up the screen shown below. There are two windows inside of this window. The one to left shows you what theme you

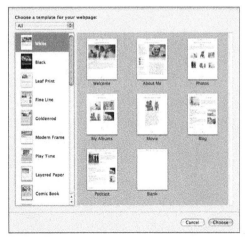

want to use. On the right, you can chose what format you want to use – Welcome, About Me, Photos, etc. Note – after you start a site – iWeb always brings up that site when launched again. You have to select a New site to start over.

iWeb – Main Screen

Below is a sample of the main work environment of iWeb. Notice that I chose a Photos template and that shows up under **Site** all the way on the upper left corner. Photos currently are the one and only webpage in my site. The white area (can be different if you chose a different theme) is the preview of the webpage. The icons with a black background behind them make up the Media section of the program. I will go over the other elements on the pages to follow.

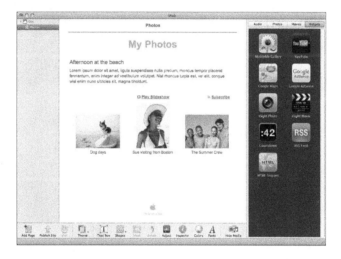

 This button adds another page to your site. It brings up the theme and template chooser shown on the previous page.

By default, this button sends your site to **MobileMe** and publishes it (makes it visible to the outside world). You can setup **MobileMe** to use another domain (added cost to you). This maybe wise or necessary – depending on your needs. Below is the dialog box that comes up when your site is done being published. Notice that is gives you the actual web address (http://web.me.com/gdurdik/site) and that you can announce it the world in an email by clicking on Announce.

 This button just brings up the current "live" site on the web.

This button allows you to bring up the themes and change the one you have. To the right is a sample of all of the themes available to you.

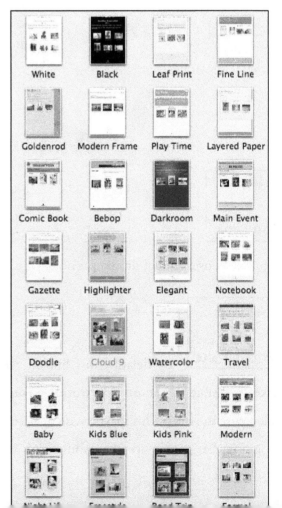

This button allows you to create a free-floating text box.

 This button allows inserting a variety of shapes. A sample of a few of them is shown to right.

This button allows hiding or masking part of the image in your webpage. An example of this is shown below. The lighter area around the photo will be removed when the mask is applied.

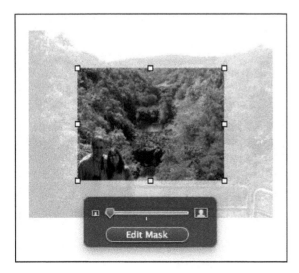

This does what it says – it rotates your graphic 90 degrees at a time.

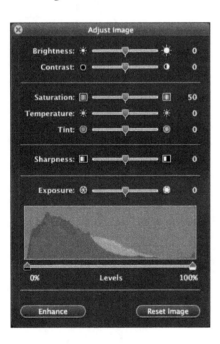 The **adjust button** allows you to modify your image in a variety of ways. On the bottom left is the Enhance button. The application attempts – the best it can – to make the image look its best.

This button brings up the **Inspector dialog box.** This is shown to the right. Notice that there is a row of eight icons. Each one represents a different function. The Palm tree icon is the Photos inspector and the T is Text inspector.

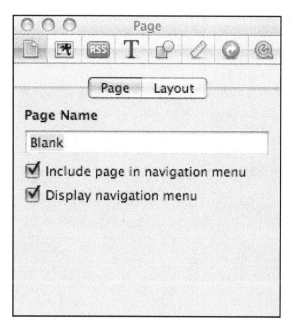

 This button brings up the color palettes you can choose. Each one is unique. A sample of one of the palettes is shown to the right.

This button deals exclusively with text. The window it brings up is shown to the right.

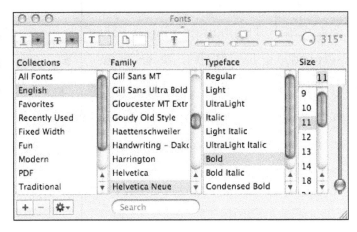

This button hides or shows the Media section of program. Media includes audio, movies, photos or widgets.

iWeb Menus

iWeb - iWeb Menu

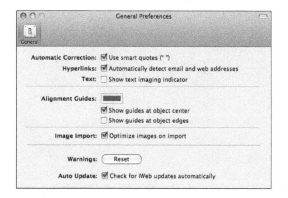

This menu contains two important items. The first is **About iWeb**. This tells you what version you are running. The second is **Preferences….** This is discussed below.

iWeb - iWeb Menu - Preferences

This menu consists of four groups of options. The first group – at the top of the screen has three options. They are **Automatic correction** – decide if you want to use smart quotes, have iWeb **automatically detect email and web addresses** and last – **show the text imaging indicator**. The second group deals with **Alignment guides**. You can set their color and decide if you want them for the object center and/or object edge. The next option deals with Image imports. By default, it will optimize images on import. This is recommended. The last group asks if you want to reset warnings and updates. You can have iWeb automatically check for updates.

iWeb – File Menu

New Page	⌘N
New Site	⇧⌘N
Close	⌘W
Save	⌘S
Revert to Saved...	
Publish Site Changes	
Publish Entire Site	
Visit Published Site	
Check for New Comments	
Submit Podcast to iTunes...	
Set Up Google AdSense...	
Set Up Personal Domain on MobileMe	
Page Setup...	⇧⌘P
Print...	⌘P

In this menu you can create a new Page or Site, save your work, publish new site changes or the entire site. You also visit the published site here as well. You can setup **Google Adsense...** and a personal Domain on **MobileMe**. Last, you can print your work as well.

iWeb – Edit Menu

Undo Unmask	⌘Z
Redo	⇧⌘Z
Cut	⌘X
Copy	⌘C
Paste	⌘V
Paste and Match Style	⌥⇧⌘V
Delete	
Delete Page	
Duplicate	⌘D
Select All	⌘A
Deselect All	⇧⌘A
Find	▶
Spelling	▶
Special Characters...	⌥⌘T

Here you can **undo** the last action you preformed or **redo** it if you decide to keep the change. You can **Cut** items out of you work, **Copy** items found in your work and **Paste** copied items into your site. **Paste and Match Style** will paste what is copied – exactly. You **Delete** an object or **Delete a whole page**. You **Duplicate** an item here as well. Use **Select all** if you want to make perhaps a change to the font on the whole page. You have access to a search tool via the **Find** command and a spell check via **Spelling**. Last, you have access to **Special Characters**. That is – symbols or graphics found in a font that you would not normally see.

iWeb – Insert Menu

Simply, this menu gives you the option to insert a variety of items into you document. This includes Hyperlinks, text boxes, shapes, a button or a widget. Choose… gives you access to an item not listed above.

iWeb – Format Menu

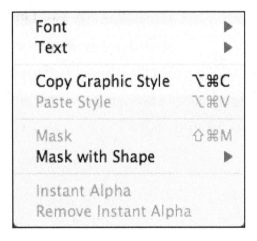

This menu allows you to modify Font and Text characteristics. You can copy a Graphic Style, Mask a picture or Mask with a shape. Last, you have the option to use Instant Alpha – which attempts to make the color you chose in a picture transparent.

iWeb – Arrange Menu

Bring Forward	⌥⇧⌘F
Bring to Front	⇧⌘F
Send Backward	⌥⇧⌘B
Send to Back	⇧⌘B
Align Objects	▶
Distribute Objects	▶
Rotate Clockwise	⌥⌘R
Rotate Counter Clockwise	⌘R
Flip Horizontally	
Flip Vertically	

This menu is broken down into four sections. In the first section we have **Bring Forward, Bring to Front, Send Backward or Send to Back.** Think of your document as having many layers to it. Each graphic or item has its own layer. Let's say there is a text box with a short sentence in it. You want to put a picture behind it. Make sure that the picture is over the text and select either Send Backward or Send to Back. After this is done, your text is on visible on the screen and the picture is the background for it. The next section allows you to **align objects – Left, Center, or right, Top, Middle or bottom.** You can **distribute objects vertically or horizontally**. The next section simply allows you to decide how you want to **rotate an image**. The last option on this menu allows you to **Flip an image Horizontally or Vertically**.

iWeb – View Menu

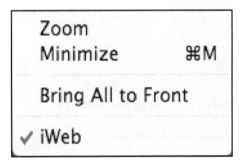

Show Layout – shows the invisible guides in you webpage. **Inspector** – show or hide – is a tool to modify many characteristics of you website. You can also have iWeb show the **Colors palette**, or **Adjust image tool**. Last, you can have iWeb hide the Media section of your main window. In the example I used earlier – the Media section is showing.

iWeb – Window Menu

Zoom – Makes the window as large as it can on your screen. **Minimize** – shrinks you work and places an icon of it in your Dock. Click on this icon to bring your work back on the screen. **Bring All to Front** – If you have many applications open at once – this option will bring all open windows associated with iWeb and bring them in front of all other windows.

iWeb – Help Menu

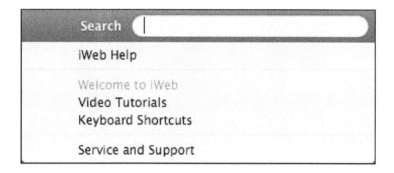

I am not a webmaster. I hopefully provided enough info to get your feet wet and start creating a site. If you have further questions or want to watch more in-depth video tutorials – use this menu.

So.... Got something you want to world to see or hear about? Photos or Resume or Product? iWeb is a great application to get started creating simple to complex web pages. Start small – Think Big when it comes to creating your website.

iLife

GarageBand

Want to be the next rock star? GarageBand is an awesome tool to create your own music. It even now offers lessons to help you learn certain instruments. As with the other applications I touched upon – I will go over the working environment and the GarageBand menus. So, let's get started with the default startup screen. As you will notice from the screen shown to the right – you have access to a Getting Started Video or video tutorials.

Click on close when you want to get the party started.

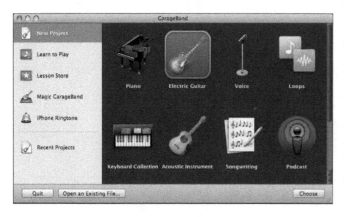

The next screen – shown to the left – is the access point to a variety of ways to use Garageband. If you just want to start composing – click on **New Project** and choose what instrument or type of project.

(Songwriting or Podcast). I will go over in great detail (I am not musician so I will keep things as simple as I can) the main environment of a new project. But first... I will go over the other cool and exciting things you can do with GarageBand.

Learn to Play

Here GarageBand gives you access to a sample piano or guitar lesson.

Lesson Store

Here you can purchase additional lessons for GarageBand. It includes Basic lessons and Artist lessons (shown above).

Magic GarageBand

Prefer jammin' with a band? Magic GarageBand creates a band atmosphere for all of the types of music shown in the screen above.

I chose FUNK. Notice that the Piano has a spotlight on it and it states it my instrument. This means when you are jammin' – you will be the pianist.

Notice the **My Instrument** section on the bottom left of the screen. Do you see the

little tuning fork? If you click on it – it turns blue. This will then give you

access to the keys shown in the example above. Note – you can have GarageBand

play a snippet or the Entire Song.

 The big red button starts recording your piece.

This is the PLAY button.

 After you done jammin' you can have the piece

brought into the main editing window and further edit your work.

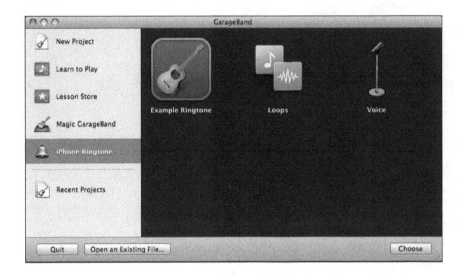

iPhone Ringtone – Create your own ringtones and send them to iTunes.

Back to creating a new masterpiece via New Project.

The first screen you will see is the one to the right. Notice that you have to give it a name and designate where it is to be saved.   In the section below you decide what the tempo is going to be, set a Signature and Key.

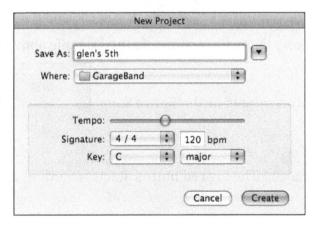

GarageBand Main Window

There are two main sections. The first is the **Track list** – (Grand Piano name and icon in the example above. The section below is where you compose the notes – **Track editor**. Note the piano keys – this is what you use to create your songs. Below is an example of a window with notes already entered into the composition. Beethoven I am not.

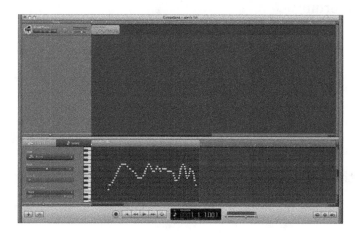

I just want to elaborate on the track controls a bit. Notice that the image above has a green tint to it. This means that the instrument is selected and the options for it can be adjusted.

The Red Circle – enables or disables recording on the selected track.

The Speaker Icon – mutes or "unmutes" the track.

The Headphones Icon – solos or "unsolos" the track. (All other instruments are turned off)

The Lock Icon – locks or unlocks a track. It also renders it to your hard drive, which frees up processing power.

Down Arrow Icon – shows or hides automation for a track.

Space Bar – Pauses playback or recording.

This button creates a **New Track**. You are given the choice of a **software instrument, real instrument or electric guitar**. This is shown to the right.

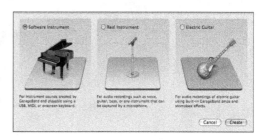

IF you chose a **Software Instrument** – the following window is displayed on the right side of your working environment. Chose the instrument you want and just click on it. It will then appear as "Shimmering Flute" inside your Track list for example.

 This button shows or hides the Track editor.

 This button is the record button.

 These buttons deal with maneuvering around inside your track. Arrow pointing to the left with a line next to it – brings you back to the beginning of your work. The DOUBLE Arrows advances your track forward or backward. The big triangle in the middle is the PLAY button. The arrows in a circular motion – turns cycling on or off. If it is on – GarageBand will cycle only the music already composed. It will get to the end of the section and then go back to the beginning and start over.

 This "LCD" screen shows you the measures (and other items via the Control Menu) found in you work.

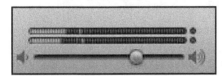 This shows you the left and right volumes and gives you to change the volume with the slider on the bottom.

This button brings up the Loop Browser. The choices are shown below.

 This button displays track info. It hides or shows other options or features of Garageband that is displayed on the right hand side of the main window.

 This button brings on the **Media Browser**. This is shown to the right. Notice that you have access to **Audio**, **Photos and Movies**. There is a search feature located at the bottom of the screen.

GarageBand Menus

GarageBand – GarageBand Menu

About GarageBand	
Preferences...	⌘,
Shop for GarageBand Products	
Provide GarageBand Feedback	
Register GarageBand	
Check for Updates...	
Learn about Jam Packs	
Services	▶
Hide GarageBand	⌘H
Hide Others	⌥⌘H
Show All	
Quit GarageBand	⌘Q

This menu contains a few important items. **About GarageBand** states what version you are running. **Preferences...** are discussed on the next page. **Shop for GarageBand Products** brings you to an Apple store website dealing with items for this product. You can look elsewhere for similar items not found there. **Check for Updates** – goes online and checks to see if there are any updates. **Learn about Jam Packs** – you can purchase more loops and more instruments via the website it brings up.

GarageBand – GarageBand Menu Preferences - General

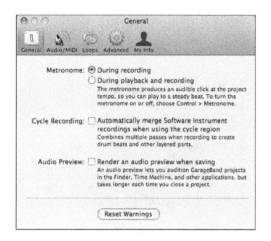

Metronome can be set to be on only during recording or recording and playback mode. **Cycle Recording** – can be set to automatically merge software instruments inside the cycle region. **Audio Preview** – creates an audio preview that can be used in the Finder, Time Machine and other apps.

GarageBand – GarageBand Menu Preferences – Audio/MIDI

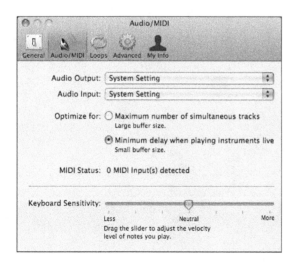

Audio Output can be set for System Setting or Built-in Output. **Audio Input** can be set for System Setting, Built-in Microphone or Built-in Input. You can have GarageBand be optimized for a large number of simultaneous tracks (large buffer size) or have a minimum delay when playing instruments live (small buffer size).

If you have a MIDI device attached

it would show up next to MIDI Status. Last, you can set keyboard sensitivity. The default is neutral.

GarageBand – GarageBand Menu Preferences – Audio/MIDI

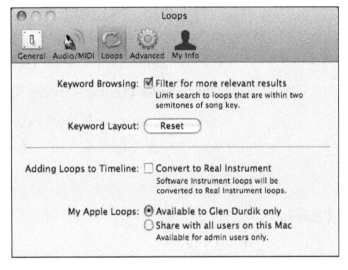

You can have **Keyword Browsing** filter for more relevant results (loops that are within two semitones of song key). You reset the **Keyword Layout** if you wish. You are given the option her to convert added loops to Real Instruments. Last, you can make you Apple loops only available to you or share with other (admin) users on your Mac.

GarageBand – GarageBand Menu Preferences – Advanced

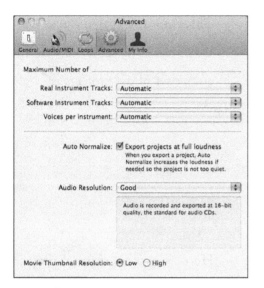

Here you can set the maximum number of Real Instrument Tracks **(8-255)**, Software Instrument Tracks **(8-64)** and Voices per Instrument **(10 sampled, 5 other to 64 sampled, max other)**. **Auto Normalize** – if GarageBand thinks a part of your project is to soft (quiet) it will increase the loudness. **Audio Resolution** – Good is the default – standard for audio CDs. It can also be Better and Best. Best records and exports at 24-Bits.

GarageBand – GarageBand Menu Preferences – My Info

This option will determine what Playlist is to be used and who the composer of the projects is.

GarageBand – File Menu

Here you can create a project, open a saved work, open recent work, close the work or save or perform a **Save As...** If you perform a **Save As...,** you can also Archive the Project (this saves Real Instrument Apple loops into the project so that the project can be safely moved to another Mac) or use Compact Project (this saves a 128kbps AAC format to reduce the size of the file).

GarageBand – Edit Menu

Undo Recording	⌘Z
Redo	⇧⌘Z
Cut	⌘X
Copy	⌘C
Paste	⌘V
Delete	
Delete and Move	^⌫
Select All	⌘A
Add Marker	P
Split	⌘T
Join	⌘J
Add To Loop Library...	
Special Characters...	⌥⌘T

In this menu – you can **undo** the last action taken or **redo** it if you decide to keep the change. **Cut** – removes item you have highlighted. **Copy** – takes what you highlighted and puts it in the System "clipboard" for future use. **Paste** – Put what you just copied in the work at the place you have chosen. **Delete** – removes the item you highlighted. **Delete and Move** – deletes and allows you to move the item elsewhere. **Select All** – highlights all tracks and all the notes housed in them. **Add Marker** – allows you to add special markers for podcasts or movie projects. **Split** – allows you to take a portion of your work and play it from a spot different then the beginning of the track. **Add to Loop Library** – you can take you selection and put into the Loop Library which can be used in other projects. **Special Characters** - Adds access to special symbols not normally seen when use fonts.

GarageBand – Track Menu

Hide Track Info	⌘I
Show Arrange Track	⇧⌘A
Show Master Track	⌘B
Show Podcast Track	⇧⌘B
Show Movie Track	⌥⌘B
New Track...	⌥⌘N
Delete Track	⌘⌫
Duplicate Track	⌘D
New Basic Track	⇧⌘N
Fade Out	

This menu allows you to chose what Tracks you want to show. This includes Arrange, Master, Podcast and Movie. You can add, delete or Duplicate a track here as well. **Fade Out** – allows you to have the track volume slowly decrease to silence.

GarageBand – Control Menu

✓ Metronome	⌘U
Count In	⇧⌘U
✓ Snap to Grid	⌘G
Show Alignment Guides	⇧⌘G
Ducking	⇧⌘R
Show Loop Browser	⌘L
Show Media Browser	⌘R
Hide Editor	⌘E
Show Chord in LCD	⌘F
Show Time in LCD	⇧⌘F
✓ Show Measures in LCD	⌥⌘F
Show Tempo in LCD	^⌘F
Lock Automation Curves to Regions	⌥⌘A

This menu deals with several different items. You can have the **Metronome** and **Count In** showing. **Ducking** is used to lower track volumes so that voices can be heard better. Good for Podcasts. You can show or hide various elements. This includes the Loop and Media Browser; the LCD is the blue digital readout in your main window. You can have Chords, Time, Measures and Tempo shown in this LCD display if you wish. **Lock automation Curves to**

Regions - each track has automation curves for various settings. Here you can specify and lock in these curves,

GarageBand – Share Menu

Send Song to iTunes
Send Ringtone to iTunes
Send Podcast to iWeb
Send Movie to iDVD

Export Song to Disk...

Burn Song to CD

Ready to share your work with the rest of your fans? Here you can send a song or ringtone to iTunes. You can send a Podcast to iWeb to be part of a website. You can burn a song to a CD. You can export your song as an MP3 or AAC format.

GarageBand – Window Menu

Minimize   ⌘M
Zoom

Keyboard   ⌘K
Musical Typing   ⇧⌘K

✓ glen's 5th.band

Minimize – takes the current window and removes from your monitor and places it into your Dock. To get it back on the screen – click on the icon in the Dock. **Zoom** – makes the window the largest it can be on your screen.

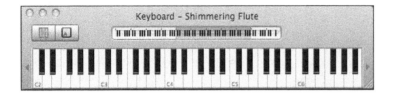

To the left – is the keyboard when you chose Keyboard in this Window Menu

To the left is the interface when you chose Musical Typing in the Window Menu.

GarageBand – Help Menu

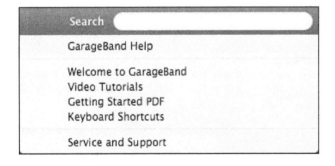

Got a question not answered in this short guide – go to this menu for the answer. You can type in a topic question, view Video Tutorials, a Welcome Video or view a Getting Started PDF.

So…when will I hear your new song on the radio?? I hope that I got you feet wet in using GarageBand. I am not a musician – so this program is still a mystery in some aspects. I do think it is a great tool to start learning how to write music for the beginner and a good tool for the more experienced to lay down some mean tunes.

iLife

iTunes

iTunes started a revolution – music downloads started to soar after Apple introduced iTunes and the iTunes Store. iTunes is also available for Windows users

as well. You just got your new Mac and want to create an audio library of all your CDs. You might want to purchase a song you just heard on the radio. iTunes provides the solution to both of these situations. I will go over all the elements of iTunes in the next few pages. However,

when you first launch iTunes – there are a few questions that have to be answered before you can begin importing or purchasing. The first screen that arises is the

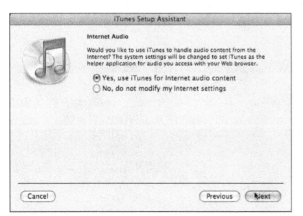

welcome screen. This is shown above. Click next to move on. The next screen – shown to the left asks if you want to use iTunes for Internet audio content. This should be set to Yes for most users. There are other Internet audio applications that must be downloaded and installed to see or hear the content in some websites.

The next screen shown to the right asks if you want iTunes to import content that you already have stored on your hard drive. Notice that it only searches your Home Folder – you may have content elsewhere that you may want to add later.

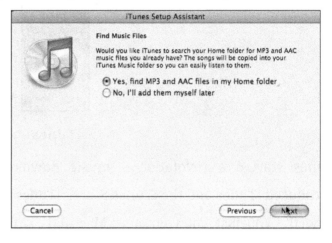

The next screen – shown to the left asks if you want to keep your music folder organized. Most users will keep this on an say Yes. It makes it easier to find you content in searches if the info was changed automatically.

The last screen that arises deals with album artwork. Basically, if you want an albums' artwork to be part of your library – you have to create and iTunes store account. It is free – but requires a credit card

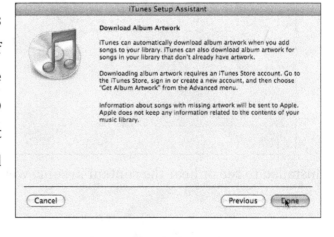

account to start.

iTunes – Main Windows

Music

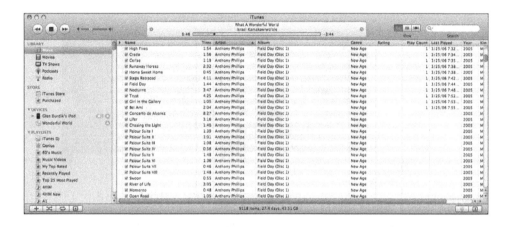

Above is the window you will see if you click on MUSIC under LIBRARY on the top left side of the iTunes main window. Note the two items under DEVICES – Glen Durdik's iPod and Wonderful World. If you have an iPod (which I will describe in detail later) this is where it would show up. Wonderful World is a CD and it too would show up under Devices.

Movies

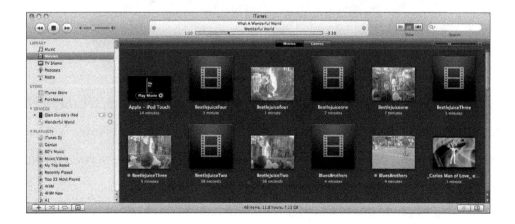

Above is the window you will see if you click on MOVIES under LIBRARY on the top left side of your iTunes main window.

TV Shows

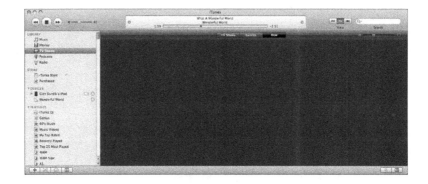

Above is the screen you will see if you click on TV SHOWS under LIBRARY. It is broken down into three categories – TV Shows, Genres and New.

Podcasts

Above is the screen you will see if you click on PODCASTS under Library. Note that is broken down into three categories – Podcasts, Categories and New. Note also that you have access to a Podcast Directory at the lower right of the screen and that you can unsubscribe to Podcasts here as well.

Radio

Above is the screen you will see if you click on RADIO under LIBRARY. This gives you access to list of streaming radio streams in one convenient location. Under each heading (Blues, Classic Rock) is a list of stations, their bit rate (higher number better = better audio quality, but more data to download causing it to be slower or pause) and a description of the station.

Store

The next category after LIBRARY is STORE. This is where you can download music, TV Shows and Movies. In the example above, I searched for the group "GENESIS."

Notice that is brought items in various categories such as ARTISTS, ALBUMS and MUSIC VIDEOS. Below that lists all the songs and other items in a basic straight list. The next item - Purchased is not shown here. All items purchased via iTunes go into this folder. You can then drag them into a new playlist or one that already exists.

Note: When you download an item – the Downloads window is shown below Purchased. The spinning arrows mean it is downloading. The number next to it displays how many items you are currently downloading. This is show on the next page.

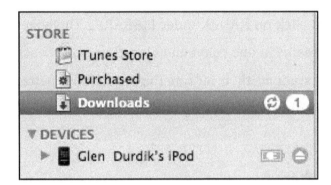

DEVICES

If you insert a CD or attach an iPod – this is where these items will show up. I will go over iPod (touch) features later on. You can import a CD by clicking on the IMPORT CD icon on the bottom right of the screen.

PLAYLISTS – iTUNES DJ

Above is the first screen you will see if you first click on iTunes DJ.   If you click on continue, the playlist iTunes has started off with is shown. An example of this is shown below.

To change the default settings, click on Settings... on the bottom right of your DJ window.

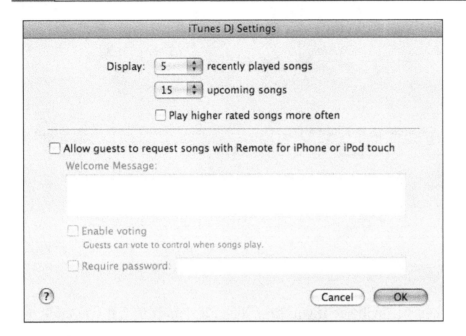

This screen is divided into two sections. The first determines what you want displayed in the iTunes window. This includes recently played songs and upcoming songs. If you decided to rate your songs - you can also have higher rated ones played more often. The second deals with accessing iTunes via an iPhone or iPod Touch. You can turn this feature on or off, enable voting and give a password to access to the DJ list.

Playlist – Genius

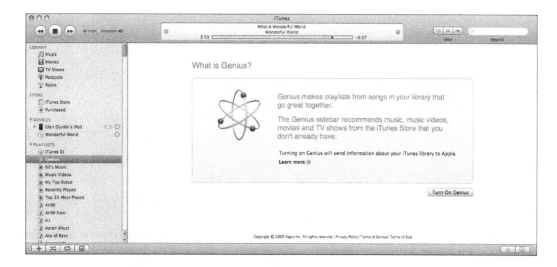

Want to find music from artists you never heard of that fits your music tastes? Enter Genius. Once setup – iTunes will suggest songs available in the store that you might like based on your library. Above is the first screen you will see when setting Genius up.

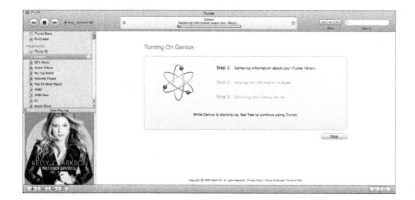

The next steps are shown above – Gather info, send to Apple, and get results.

After it is setup, just click on a song (In Your Eyes) in the example above and click on

the Genius Button on the bottom right of the screen to show what iTunes

thinks what you might like in your Library.

The button next to Genius Button is the Genius Sidebar Button. This brings up music found in the iTunes store (for purchase) that you might like to also. This is shown below.

Playlist – User Created

All other playlists are shown in the examples above are created by myself. I chose to create playlists based on an artist's name.

Views Available to view Media

List View

This view is the most comprehensive option. Notice that it gives the Name, Time, Artist, Album by Artist, Genre and Rating (and more not shown above). This is what is on by default. You can add Release Date, or sample rate for example.

Grid View

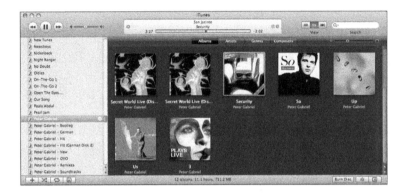

This option is not as descriptive as the List View. Albums are displayed by their cover art. If you click on the album you like, you are given a similar List View – but with a small picture of the cover art of the album on the left.

Cover Flow View

This is the most visual of the three views. Notice there is a slider below the album cover shown up. You navigate the playlist by dragging this slider back and forth. The contents of the highlighted album are shown below in a list view.

Main Window – Icons not previous mentioned

 Red (far right) closes the window. Yellow (middle) shrinks the window into the Dock. Click on the icon in the Dock to bring it back to full size. Green (far right) - Makes the window as large as possible or displays just the basics – a "MiniPlayer" shown below.

 When clicked, it brings you first to the beginning of the track playing. If you continue to click it – it will go backwards down the playlist.

 Plays the track you have currently selected. If music is playing – the Play button turns into a Pause button.

 This button skips to the next song in the playlist.

 This slider determines the volume in iTunes. You might have to adjust the system volume to get the volume you want. (System maybe set too low or too high)

This window shows the time elapsed, Title of the Song, Artist, Album and time remaining of the song currently playing. You also have access to the Genius feature here.

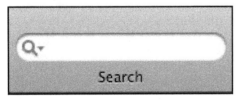 Mentioned in previous section.

 Here you can search for an item in your Library. Note – you have to have the category under LIBRARY to search the entire Library. Otherwise, you are just searching within the current playlist.

 This button creates a new Playlist.

 This button turns a Shuffle feature ON or OFF.

This button is the Repeat button. By default it is turned off. If you click on it once, you get a blue symbol , which means it will repeat the entire Playlist. If you click on it a second time, you get a blue symbol with a Number 1 inside of it . This will repeat only the currently playing song. If you click it a third time – you turn off the repeat feature.

This button hides or shows Album Covers in the Playlist section of the iTunes main window.

9118 items, 27.4 days, 43.51 GB This section on the bottom – in the middle – displays the total items in a playlist, the number of hours (and days) it would take to listen to the entire playlist and the actual hard drive space the playlist takes.

Burn Disc If you want to make a copy of your songs or playlists – choose the item and click on Burn Disc. The following window will appear...

Notice that you can burn Audio CDs (works with all CD players), MP3 CDs – some CD players and computers or a Data CD or DVD. An MP3 CD can store a whole lot more music that a regular CD, but may not work in older CD players. A Data disc will 99% of the time only work on a computer.

iTunes – Menus

iTunes – iTunes Menu

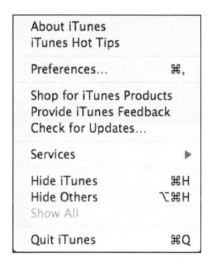

There are a few important items in this menu. **About iTunes** – tells you want version you are running. **Preferences...** are discussed next. **Check for Updates** goes online and checks for any updates for the software.

iTunes – iTunes Menu – Preferences - General

Here you give your Library a name. This is important if you share your Library over a network. **Show:** Decides what is displayed on the left-hand side of the iTunes Window. **Note:** If you have and iPod Touch or iPhone – you should have Applications set to SHOW. Insert CD settings and Import Settings are discussed on the next page. You should have iTunes automatically retrieve CD track names and check for software updates.

✓ Show CD
Begin Playing
Ask To Import CD
Import CD
Import CD and Eject

The options to the left are the options you have when you insert a CD into your computer. Show CD is the default choice.

Import Settings

Import Using: MP3 Encoder

Setting: High Quality (160 kbps)

Details

80 kbps (mono)/160 kbps (stereo), joint stereo, optimized for MMX/SSE, using MP.

☐ Use error correction when reading Audio CDs

Use this option if you experience problems with the audio quality from Audio CDs. This may reduce the speed of importing.

Note: These settings do not apply to songs downloaded from the iTunes Store.

Cancel   OK

Import Settings – There are two items to consider here. The first is what Encoder you want to use. I chose MP3 as my choice as I like to make custom MP3s CDs from my Library. Some of the other Encoders offer higher quality sound however.

AAC Encoder
AIFF Encoder
Apple Lossless Encoder
✓ MP3 Encoder
WAV Encoder

These are the choices for Encoder. Each has it's strengths and weaknesses. For ease of use of burning CDs I chose MP3.

Good Quality (128 kbps)
✓ High Quality (160 kbps)
Higher Quality (192 kbps)

Custom...

The Next step is the Setting for the Encoder. The example to the left is for MP3 encoding. The higher the kbps the better the sound quality.

iTunes – iTunes Menu – Preferences -
Playback

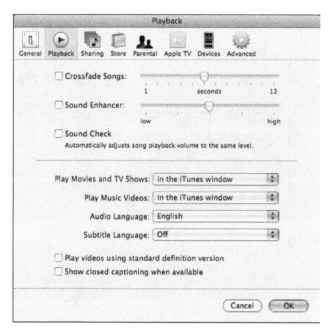

The first three settings (**Cross fade, Sound Enhancer and Sound Check**) modify the way the music is played. I have never used the Sound Enhancer – so try it and see if you like it. Sound Check is nice in that it keeps the volume at certain level. Play Movies and TV Shows and Play Music Videos can be either the iTunes window or

> in artwork viewer
> ✓ in the iTunes window
> in a separate window
> full screen
> full screen (with visuals)

You can set the Audio Language, have Subtitles turner on, play videos in standard definition and last – show close captioning when available.

iTunes – iTunes Menu – Preferences - Sharing

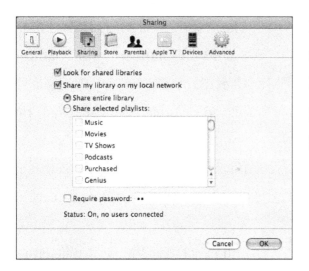

If you are a network – you can search for shared libraries or share your own. Note that you can share just selected playlists and that you can assign it a password.

iTunes – iTunes Menu – Preferences - Store

The top part of this window deals with the way you purchase your media from the store. Buy and download using 1-Click will purchase you item(s) by just confirming your purchase. The second – places the items in a traditional Shopping Cart and is only purchased when you click on Buy Now. In the lower half, you can have iTunes automatically check for downloads, automatically download prepurchased content and last – check for and download missing album artwork.

iTunes – iTunes Menu – Preferences – Parental

Want to block your little ones for harsh media? Use this preference to modify what they can see or download. The first section disables – if you want – Podcasts, Radio, iTunes Store or Shared Libraries. The second section sets what are the age limits for movies, TV shows and games. You can also set a broader category by restricting explicit content. **Note: DO NOT** forget to lock this preference after you are done setting it up. Hey – kids are smart these days.

iTunes – iTunes Menu – Preferences – Apple TV

If you own an Apple TV – this is where you would set it up to link with your iTunes.

iTunes – iTunes Menu – Preferences – Devices

iTunes makes a backup of your devices before it performs updates. Note that I have one device and one backup in the list. You can disable iTunes from automatically syncing iPhones and iPods here as well. You can have the program look for remote speakers connected via AirTunes, disable iTunes control over remote speakers and allow iTunes to take control over remote speakers. Last, you can disable iTunes from looking for iPhone or iPod Touch Remotes.

iTunes – iTunes Menu – Preferences – Advanced

The first section of this window deals with the Music Folder. Note that there is a default location, but it CAN be changed to another one if you prefer. Next, I would leave the default choice of keeping the iTunes Music folder organized and to automatically copy files to the iTunes Music folder when adding an item to the library. Next, you have three options to ponder. The streaming buffer size determines the size of the file to be streamed. iTunes probably is your best bet for Internet playback for most of your needs, so leave it Set to use iTunes. Reset all dialog warnings – clears all warnings. When you minimize iTunes – you get a

MiniPlayer. If you click on the "Keep MiniPlayer on top..." This player will always be the top (visible) window on your monitor. The same reasoning applies for the movie window option. The **Visualizer** is a cool feature that syncs music to an ever-changing visual image. By default it is only shown in the iTunes window. Here you can make it the full screen. Grouping of compilations when browsing is the last option here.

iTunes – File Menu

New Playlist	⌘N
New Playlist from Selection	⇧⌘N
New Playlist Folder	
New Smart Playlist...	⌥⌘N
Edit Smart Playlist	
Close Window	⌘W
Add to Library...	⌘O
Library	▶
Get Info	⌘I
Rating	▶
Show in Finder	⌘R
Show Duplicates	
Sync iPod	
Transfer Purchases from iPod	
Page Setup...	
Print...	⌘P

Here you can create a **New Playlist** (no contents), a **Playlist from a selection** of songs or create a **Smart Playlist**. A **Smart Playlist** will take items from you library based on your criteria. **Get Info** – gives you details on the item you highlighted. You can also rate your selection here as well. Show in Finder brings up the window of the actual location of your song. You can Sync your iPod here if it is not done automatically and transfer purchases made away from your Mac on your iPod.

These are the options found in the Library Submenu. Note that you can backup your entire library to a disc or export it as well. Also you can burn a Playlist to disc here.

Back Up to Disc...
Consolidate Library...
Export Library...

Burn Playlist to Disc
Import Playlist...
Export Playlist...

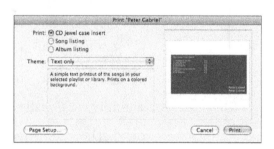

This is the screen that comes up when you select Print. You print a CD Jewel case insert – shown on the left, Song listings or Album Listing. The themes that can be printed are shown below.

✓ Text only
Mosaic
White mosaic
Single cover
Text only (Black & White)
Mosaic (Black & White)
Single side (Black & White)
Large playlist (Black & White)

iTunes – Edit Menu

Undo	⌘Z
Cut	⌘X
Copy	⌘C
Paste	⌘V
Delete	
Select All	⌘A
Select None	⇧⌘A
Special Characters...	

This Edit Menu is similar to other Edit menus. You can **undo** or **redo** an action, have access to **Cut** and **Delete**, **Copy** and **Paste** functions. You can also use **Select All** to highlight all items shown in the main window (usually a playlist). **Special Characters** allows having access to characters found in fonts that are not normally seen.

iTunes – View Menu

✓ as List	⌥⌘3
as Grid	⌥⌘4
as Cover Flow	⌥⌘5
View Options...	⌘J
Show Current Song	⌘L
Show Browser	⌘B
Show Genius Sidebar	⇧⌘G
Show Artwork Column	⌘G
Video Size	▶
Visualizer	▶
Show Visualizer	⌘T
Full Screen	⌘F

The first three options are List, Grid or Cover Flow. I showed what these are earlier in this guide. View Options are shown below the Edit Menu. If you are jumping around iTunes while listening to a song – the playlist window will reflect where you are looking. If you select **Show Current Song** – it returns the window back to the playlist the song is located. An example of Show Browser and Genius Sidebar are shown below and on the next page. Show Artwork column just adds the album cover to the current Playlist.

View Options.

This is what the playlist window looks like if you have the Browser showing. It has Genre, Artist and Albums on top of the playlist currently in use.

This is what the Genius Sidebar looks like.

Video Size can be any of the sizes shown on the left.

The Visualizer is a cool feature that syncs various shapes and colors with the song you are playing. iTunes has more than one choice and you can download others. An example is shown to the left. Note – by default it only plays in the iTunes window. You can have it play Full Screen by choosing the last item in this menu.

iTunes – Controls Menu

Stop	space
Next	⌘ ⋯→
Previous	⌘ ←⋯
Next Chapter	⇧⌘ ⋯→
Previous Chapter	⇧⌘ ←⋯
Audio & Subtitles	▶
Shuffle	▶
Repeat	▶
Eject Disc	⌘E

The first item here is very useful to remember. To stop a song or video – hit the SPACE BAR. Next and Previous – go forward one track or back one track. Next or Previous Chapter deals with Audiobooks. Audio and Subtitles with videos. Eject Disc just removes the CD from your computer.

Turn On Shuffle
✓ By Songs
By Albums
By Groupings

Shuffle Submenu - can be also done for songs by clicking on the [⤭] button.

Off
✓ All
One

Repeat Submenu – can also be done by clicking once for All and twice for one on the [↻] button.

iTunes – Store Menu

```
Back                                    ⌘[
Forward                                 ⌘]
Home                                   ⇧⌘H
Search...

Turn Off Genius
Update Genius

Create an iMix...
Create Ringtone...

Authorize Computer...
Deauthorize Computer...

Sign Out
View My Account (phoenix737@nyc.rr.com)...
Check for Available Downloads...
```

This first part of this menu deals with Navigating through the iTunes store. Next it deals with the Genius feature of iTunes as this involves the store for suggestions to buy. An **iMix** allows you to share a Playlist with the rest of the world. You can only create a Ringtone for your phone from songs purchased from the iTunes store. **Authorize or Deauthorize Computer** – you can only have up to five computers under one iTunes account. For most people this is not a problem – but **REMEMBER to DEAUTHORIZE your computer before you erase the hard drive or give it to someone else.** iTunes stores hidden data and erased that account will be permanently ON that Mac or PC. You can sign in, sign out and check your iTunes account here as well. Check for available downloads – if you have items not yet downloaded to your computer – this option will find them and resume the download.

iTunes – Advanced Menu

Open Audio Stream...	⌘U
Subscribe to Podcast...	
Create iPod or iPhone Version	
Create Apple TV Version	
Create MP3 Version	
Get Album Artwork	
Get CD Track Names	
Submit CD Track Names	
Join CD Tracks	
Deauthorize Audible Account...	

If you know the website (url) of streaming audio – this is where you can access it. You can subscribe to Podcasts in this menu. The next section of the menu deals with converting media to work with Apple's portable devices (iPhone or iPod) or an Apple TV. If you want to create large MP3 CD from songs not in the MP3 format – this menu allows you to convert them here. Note that you will have the original and the MP3 version in your library. If you want to delete one or the other – I suggest that you add KIND to the view options and do a

Search for the item and delete the one you no longer need. **Get Album Artwork** and **Get CD Track Names** go out via iTunes to search for the items you are missing. Some items may NOT be found. You can add (Submit) CD track names here if you wish. Join CD tracks takes out the spaces between songs normally put in when importing. Last, you can deauthorize and Audible Account here.

iTunes – Window Menu

Minimize	⌘M
Zoom	^⌘Z
✓ iTunes	⌥⌘1
Equalizer	⌥⌘2
Bring All to Front	

Minimize – shrinks the current window and places it in the Dock. To get it back – click on the icon in the Dock. **Zoom** – either shrinks the iTunes window to the MiniPlayer view or brings it back to its normal Player Window. If you have a lot of applications open – you can select **Bring All to Front** to bring all iTunes windows to be in front of all others.

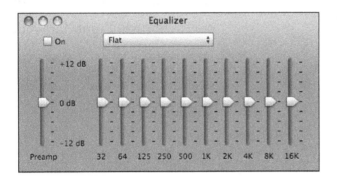

To the left is the **Equalizer** function of iTunes. There are a number of presets (Flat shown) and can be turned on or off.

iTunes – Help Menu

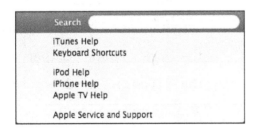

The concept of iTunes is simple. As you have seen – there are a lot of details to know about in order to fully take control of iTunes and use it effectively. I hope I covered the basics in this manual. However, if you have other questions – go to this menu for further insight or tips.

....and now to iPod use......

Using an iPod (touch) with your PC and iTunes

OK. Just got a new iPod and don't know what to do next. I have an iPod Touch so I will go over the items associated with it and iTunes. Before I begin – let me state that iTunes backs up your iPod whenever an update is made to it. The screens involved are shown below.

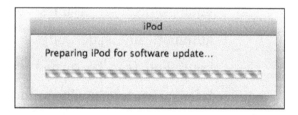

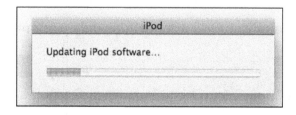

Now back to beginning – sort of. If something is wrong with your iPod or you want to just erase it and start over from scratch – there is a Restore Feature that brings you iPod back to its original settings. In order to write a more complete manual –

this is what I did to my iPod. The Restore window is shown below. Note that your brand new iPod would NOT have a backup to restore from.

If you select Setup as a new iPod – the screen below comes up after you click on

Continue. Here you can name your iPod, set iTunes to automatically sync songs to your iPod (can be turned off later), automatically add photos to the iPod (as many as it could fit) and last – automatically sync applications. Applications only work on iPod Touches and iPhones.

After this done – your iPod now shows up under DEVICES in your iTunes window. The plug inside the battery icon means it is attached and charging. The arrow pointing upwards is what you need to click when you want to remove your iPod from your Mac. Never disconnect it without doing this. It could corrupt your iPod. Bad.

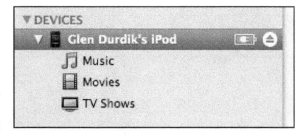

If your iPod is clicked on in the main window – the following screen will appear on the right on the main window. The window is broken down into four categories. On the top are the tabs of what type of media is on your iPod. Below that is the iPod section, which tells you the name, the capacity, the software version and serial number of your ultra-cool iPod Touch. The next section is Version. Here you will find out if your iPod needs and update or check for an update. I mentioned earlier there is a button to Restore your iPod to its original settings. If you see the example

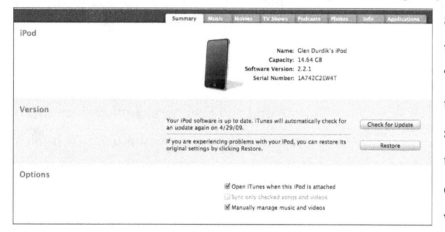

above – this is where it is found. The last section is the Options section. You have three options to configure. Do you want iTunes to open when the iPod is attached? Do you only want to sync checked songs and videos? And last – Do you want to manually manage music and videos?

Before I continue with the other tabs – let just mention that below this window is a visual bar that describes what is on the iPod and how much space is left. This is shown below.

Empty...

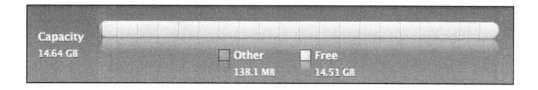

With media on it...

Capacity					
14.64 GB	Audio	Video	Photos	Apps	Other	Free
	7.69 GB	1.48 GB	378.6 MB	76.8 MB	148.1 MB	4.89 GB

One last thing – kind of important I guess. To the right of the capacity graph is the

Sync button. **Sync** iTunes does not make any changes to the iPod until you click on this button.

Music Tab

Note that you have three options here. One – do you want to Sync you music? You might want to use your iPod for videos or applications only. The next two options are – Do you want to sync ALL songs and playlists? Or Selected playlists? Many people probably have a lot more music that would fit on an iPod Touch – so selected playlists is the best option. In the example to the left – notice this is what I have selected. ALL of the items with a check mark next to them will be synced when I chose to sync my iPod.

Movies Tab

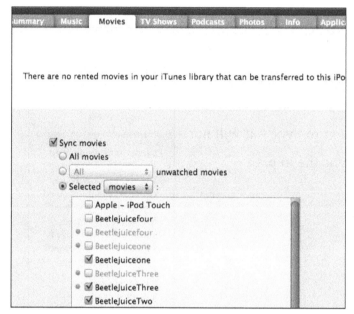

First note the cutoff message on top - you can transfer rented Movies from the iTunes store to your iPod.   This is similar to Music. Items with a check mark are synced, you can use Selected Movies or Selected Playlists, you can choose all movies or just unwatched ones.

TV Shows Tab

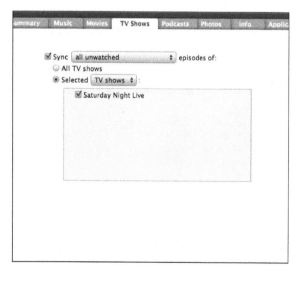

Here you can again sync all items or selected ones. You are also given the choice to NOT sync TV shows by unchecking the box next to sync. TV Shows has an interesting submenu for SYNC. This is shown to the below.

Podcasts Tab

This is similar to the other tabs – Sync ALL Or Selected. As with TV Shows, there is a custom SYNC Submenu. This is shown to the right. If you uncheck the box next to Sync – it will not sync the items.

Photos Tab

First – you are given the opportunity to sync or not sync photos. You can SYNC photos from a specific folder (shown on the left) or from iPhoto. You again can choose if you want all the items or just a selection. Note that iTunes has to optimize your photos to work on your iPod. This process is shown below.

Optimizing photos for "Glen Durdik's iPod"...
Optimizing 128 of 587

Info Tab

This tab has a lot of options to deal with. The first option is to setup **MobileMe** access. I discussed **MobileMe** in my guide to the Mac OS. You have the ability to manually sync Address Book contacts, iCal calendars and Safari bookmarks.

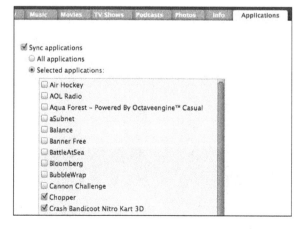

Applications Tab

Nothing new here. Choose if you want all applications or selected ones. You also given the choice to sync or don't sync applications at the very top.

So you have selected all the items you need synced and you click on the SYNC button. The following screen will appear.

Updating Files on "Glen Durdik's iPod"
Copying 816 of 1474: Last Goodbye

It is copying over 1,474 items and it is up to item number 816 in the example above.

New Features of iTunes 9

iTunes is now up to version 9.0. Most of what was covered in the previous pages of this manual. I will now go over the key differences of this new version.

New Splash Screen on Launch: There are a few new items when you iTunes first comes on your screen. This is shown below. You now have easy access to videos on variety of topics. I still prefer a paper manual that I can read at my leisure.

Home Sharing: With this new feature – you can copy purchased items to any Mac on your network. The first step is to start Home Sharing on ALL of the Macs you want connected with the SAME iTunes Store account. To activate it, go to the Advanced Menu and select Turn on Home Sharing. The screen on the next page is what pops up when you select this option.

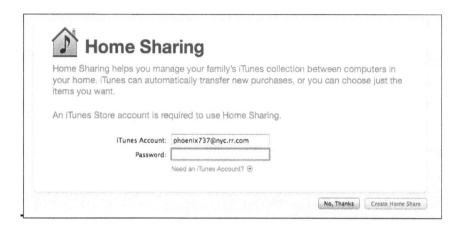

Type in your password and click on the **Create Home Share** button on the bottom right of your screen.

If you look at playlists on the left side of your screen – you will now see icons of available libraries.   There are two types of libraries. In the example above – the brown house with a musical note on it means I can copy from or to this library. Open to everything. The other icon – not shown – is blue "pages" and has a note in it. These libraries can only be read – not copied. The icon to the far right of the library (arrow pointing up) ejects this library and it is no longer connected to your library.

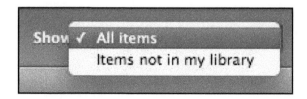

If you access a shared Home Share – there are two options of note on the bottom of the screen. The first – shown above is the **Show** button. This is on the previous page. This is on the bottom left of your screen. As you can see, if you click on it, you are given two choices. View all items or Items not in my library.

The second is **Settings**. This is found at the bottom right of your screen. Here you can set preferences as to what you want automatically transferred to your library from the library you are currently accessing. This is shown below.

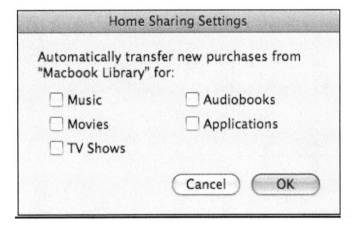

Genius Mixes – iTunes 9 builds upon the addition of the Genius function in iTunes 8. With mixes, you are given a grid with selections all based on Genius data. The Genius mix icon is shown below.

A sample Genius mix is shown below.

iTunes Store – new Interface - The iTunes store is completely different than before. Basically, explore the new items and see what you can find as usual. This is shown below.

There are a few new things that I want to highlight. One, you can now have the store go full screen. To do this, go to the iTunes menu, select Preferences, Store option. One of the choices is view store as full screen. This is show on the next page.

If you want to back to the normal view, there is a Home icon on top of the store window. Click on this icon and iTunes returns to the normal view.

On the screen, if you see an album you want more info on or purchase songs/album. Move your mouse over the album's icon and you will notice a small "i" appear on the bottom right of the icon. Click on "i" to get further info and the ability to purchase the item or songs. This is shown above.

iTunes LP/ Extras - This is an exciting new way to view music purchases. This feature is brand new and there are just a few artists that have them available for download. Think of it as purchasing a "multimedia experience" – not just a album. Special features might be unreleased videos, interviews, unreleased photos, etc.

New iPod transfer windows – iTunes has changed the way you sync data to your iPod. I selected a few to show you – so you can compare to the older version.

Music

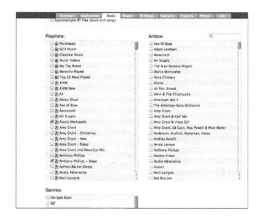

Movies

Applications

Photos

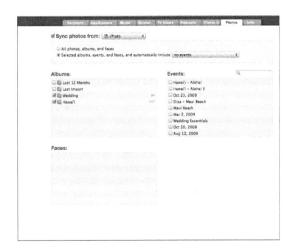

Where did the Mini-Player go?

I admit I could not figure out how to activate this feature until I did some research. Background – the Mini-player shrinks the current window to a small, minimal info window. This is show below. You normally would click the green button to shrink it or enlarge it. Not anymore. **NOTE: Update your iTunes to the latest version and the regular Mini-Player button is activated again.**

In this version of iTunes, you can either hold down the OPTION key while clicking on the green button or going to the **View** Menu and select **Switch to Mini-Player**.

Well, that iTunes is one big nutshell. I hope that you found this guide informative and plan to use iTunes in ways you have not in the past.

Final Thoughts

I hope you found my brief guide to all of the iLife applications helpful and informative. This suite of software truly allows oneself to unleash their creative side and show the world what they can do with the right tools. Some will take a few minutes become comfortable using after reading this guide. Others like iMovie and GarangeBand might take hours and hours to become productive in. I just want to add that certain tasks mentioned in this manual takes an extremely long time to perform. Exporting a completed movie project in iMovie or burning the final iDVD project to a disk is a long process. Plan on going out for a few hours or watch something on TV after starting these tasks. They may take awhile, but I am sure you will be thrilled to share your awesome movie or DVD with your friends and family!!

Legal Information

www.ingramcontent.com/pod-product-compliance
Lightning Source LLC
Chambersburg PA
CBHW080422060326
40689CB00019B/4349